KW-237-648

The Final Battle

THE DEATH OF KING ARTHUR

*Based on the story of King Arthur
by Thomas Malory*

Retold by Steve Barlow
and Steve Skidmore

HIGH RIDGE COMPREHENSIVE SCHOOL

Illustrated by Mike White

Series Editors: Steve Barlow and Steve Skidmore

Published by Ginn and Company
Halley Court, Jordan Hill, Oxford OX2 8EJ
A division of Reed Educational and Professional Publishing Ltd

Telephone number for ordering **Impact**: 01865 888084

OXFORD   MELBOURNE   AUCKLAND   JOHANNESBURG
BLANTYRE   GABORONE   IBADAN   PORTSMOUTH (NH)
USA   CHICAGO

© Steve Barlow and Steve Skidmore 1999
The moral rights of the authors have been asserted.

All rights reserved. No part of this publication may be reproduced
in any material form (including photocopying or storing it in any
medium by electronic means and whether or not transiently or
incidentally to some other use of this publication) without the
prior written permission of the copyright owner, except in
accordance with the provisions of the Copyright, Designs and
Patents Act 1988 or under the terms of a licence issued by the
Copyright Licensing Agency Ltd, 90 Tottenham Court Road,
London W1P 9HE. Applications for the copyright owner's written
permission to reproduce any part of this publication should be
addressed in the first instance to the publisher.

First published 1999

2003   2002   2001   2000   99

10 9 8 7 6 5 4 3 2 1

ISBN   0 435 21228 1

Illustrations
Mike White, Temple Rogers

Cover artwork
Lucy Weller, Début Art

Designed by Shireen Nathoo Design

Printed and bound in Great Britain by Biddles

Tel: 01865 888058   email: info.he@heinemann.co.uk

Contents

The characters

Arthur, King of Britain lives in the city of Camelot. He has a magical sword called Excalibur (Ex–*cal*–ib–er).

Queen Guinever (*Gwin*–iv–ear) is King Arthur's wife.

Sir Lancelot is a Knight of the Round Table and Queen Guinevere's lover.

Sir Gawain is a Knight of the Round Table. He has a brother called Gareth.

Merlin is a magician who looked after Arthur when he was young.

Sir Bedivere (*Bed–iv–ear*) is a Knight of the Round Table. He is loyal to King Arthur.

Mordred is King Arthur's nephew.

Sir Bors is a Knight of the Round Table and is Lancelot's friend.

5

CHAPTER 1

The Queen must die!

The Court waited in silence.

The Knights of the Round Table stood as still as statues.

The people of Camelot crowded into the Great Hall. They held their breath. Not a whisper broke the stillness.

Then …

A small figure stepped through the doorway. It was Queen Guinevere, King Arthur's wife.

The Queen walked towards the Round Table. The crowd of people moved to let her pass. She reached the Round Table and stood before King Arthur and his knights.

The Queen looked into the eyes of her husband.

"My lord," she whispered.

"Guinevere," said King Arthur sadly.

The King told the knights to sit down. Then everything was still again.

King Arthur spoke. "The Court of the Round Table is now in session. Who has a case for the Court?"

All eyes turned towards Sir Mordred. He was dressed in black and his arm hung in a sling. His face was grazed and bruised.

"I do," he said.

Arthur's eyes were filled with pain as he spoke to his nephew. "Say what you have to say, Mordred."

A great sigh ran round the Court.

"Treason is a terrible crime, Mordred," Arthur said quietly. "If the Queen is found guilty, she will be burned to death."

Mordred gave a half smile. "I know, my lord."

Arthur closed his eyes and leaned back in his chair. "The Court will hear your case."

Mordred turned to the Court and spoke.

Mordred stopped speaking as Sir Gawain slammed a fist on the table.

"You coward, Mordred! You were all armed and Lancelot had no weapon!"

The King raised his hand. "Silence, Gawain. We must hear Mordred's story."

Mordred's voice shook with anger. "He killed one of my men and stole his armour," he said. "Then he attacked my men and killed them all!"

"All except you," sneered Gawain. "You escaped. How did that happen, I wonder?"

Mordred's voice choked with bitterness. "Lancelot nearly killed me!"

Gawain leaped to his feet. "I wish he had!" he shouted.

"Silence!" Arthur commanded. "We are not here to fight. We are here for the truth."

"I came here for justice!" cried Mordred.

Arthur looked him straight in the eye. "You shall have it."

Sir Bors stood up. He was one of the King's most trusted knights.

"My lord, hear me," he said. He pointed at the Queen. "This lady has done a dreadful thing. But she is your wife and Queen. She has betrayed you. But I beg you, my lord … forgive her."

All eyes turned to Arthur.

Arthur gazed at Guinevere. The court was silent. Time seemed to stop. Finally, the King shook his head. "I cannot forgive her. She has broken the law. No one is above the law. Not even my wife."

Arthur took a deep breath. His voice rang out strong and clear. "All the Knights of the Round Table must decide what will happen to the Queen."

The King stood up. "The Court will rise."

Lay your swords on the table in front of you. If you place the handle towards the Queen, your vote is Not Guilty.

The King's voice shook. "But if you lay your sword with the point towards the Queen ..."

Arthur could not finish the sentence. He reached for his sword. The knights all drew their swords. They put them down on the Round Table with a great crash.

CHAPTER 2

King Arthur remembers

Later that night, Arthur sat in his room. He wanted to be alone. His Queen was going to be burned to death the next day.

"Why did Guinevere and Lancelot have to fall in love?" he whispered.

Arthur had trusted Lancelot most of all. He was the greatest fighter of all the Knights of the Round Table. But Lancelot had betrayed Arthur. He was a traitor.

Yet Lancelot still had many friends at Camelot. When Lancelot heard that Guinevere had been found guilty, he would try to save her life.

Arthur held his sword, Excalibur. He closed his eyes. His mind drifted back in time. Back to when he had become King …

Arthur's reign had started with another sword. Merlin the magician had set a test to find the true King of Britain. He had used his magic to put a sword in a stone.

HE WHO PULLS THIS SWORD FROM THIS STONE IS THE TRUE KING OF ALL BRITAIN

Arthur easily pulled the sword out of the stone.
He proved that he was the true King.

Arthur had used that sword until it broke in a battle. Then Merlin had taken the young King to a secret lake, to help him to find a new sword.

The Lady of the Lake gave Arthur his great sword called Excalibur.

Arthur had won many battles with Excalibur. Merlin helped him to become a good King. Arthur and his knights had brought peace and order to the land.

Then Arthur remembered the day he married Guinevere. Guinevere's father had given Arthur the Round Table as a wedding present. They had been happy times.

But now the Knights of the Round Table were growing old. Many had died in battle. Others were becoming greedy and spiteful. Even Lancelot had turned against King Arthur.

"Oh, Merlin," whispered Arthur. "If only you were here with me now."

But Merlin had disappeared many years ago. No one knew what had happened to him. Merlin could not help him now. Lancelot was a traitor and the Queen was to die.

Arthur began to weep.

CHAPTER 3

Lancelot to the rescue

Early the next morning, King Arthur sat at the Round Table. Sir Gawain stood at his side.

Mordred marched in and bowed before the King.

"We have built the bonfire," he said. "It is time for the Queen to die!"

Sir Gawain walked slowly to the window. A crowd had gathered below. They had come to see the Queen burn.

"Do you think Lancelot will come?" asked Gawain.

The King looked up. "Of course he will come. He will rescue the Queen."

Gawain nodded. "I hope so."

"Your brother, Sir Gareth, is Captain of the Guard," said Arthur. "He is Lancelot's friend. Lancelot will not hurt him."

Gawain looked worried. "Gareth is not wearing his armour. He says he will not fight Lancelot."

Arthur sighed. "I hope it will be all right."

Everything was ready for the execution.

The Queen was brought from her cell and tied to the stake. More wood was piled around her feet.

Guards with burning torches stood ready to start the fire. They turned to Mordred. Smiling, he raised his arm.

Suddenly, there was a shout of alarm. Voices cried out in panic. Lancelot had arrived!

Lancelot set the Queen free. He pulled her up onto his horse.

Mordred tried to escape, but Lancelot saw him. "Mordred!" he roared.

Gareth ran towards Lancelot, waving his arms.

"No, Lancelot," Gareth cried, "leave Mordred alone!"

But the crowd was too noisy. Lancelot did not hear his friend, Gareth. He drew his sword and charged after Mordred. He did not see Gareth in the confusion ...

Gareth's body was taken to the chapel.
Sir Gawain knelt by his dead brother and
cried. King Arthur stood behind him.

At last, Gawain turned to the King.

The King gave a deep sigh. "Lancelot will
go to his castle in France," he said. "Sir Bors
will go with him."

Gawain gripped Arthur's arm. "Lancelot
has broken your laws. He has killed my
brother. We must follow him together. He
must pay for what he has done."

I shall kill Lancelot for this.

Arthur nodded sadly. "So be it."

The King turned. "Mordred," he called softly.

Mordred came forward from the shadows.

Arthur put a hand on Mordred's shoulder. "Gawain and I must lead an army to France. I do not know how long we shall be gone. While I am away, you must rule in my place."

A smile flickered across Mordred's face. "Yes, my lord."

Arthur turned away from Mordred.
"What will become of us?" he whispered.
"Now I must fight Lancelot. He is still my
finest knight, and my best friend. My wife
will be put to death if I win. And if I lose ..."

King Arthur knelt down. "God have
mercy on us all."

CHAPTER 4

Revenge!

Lancelot and the Queen fled to Lancelot's castle in France. Arthur followed them with his army.

Lancelot and Guinevere stood on the castle walls and looked down. They were surrounded by the King's men.

"But what if you are hurt?" asked
Guinevere.

Lancelot was silent.

"And what if you meet Arthur?"

Lancelot knelt before Guinevere. "I give
you this promise. I will not fight the King.
I will not harm him. I would rather die."

Tears streamed down Guinevere's face.
"That is what I am afraid of."

32

Next morning, as the sun rose,
Lancelot led the attack.

The fighting began. Soon, the ground was soaked with the blood of men and horses.

As the battle raged, Lancelot and Gawain came face to face.

Blood poured from Gawain's wound. He looked into Lancelot's eyes. "Kill me, as you killed my brother," he snarled.

Lancelot shook his head. "There has been enough killing," he replied.

Gawain laughed through his pain. "You are not just a traitor, you are a coward," he sneered.

Lancelot glared. "No man calls me a coward!" He raised his sword above Gawain's head.

"No, Lancelot!"

Lancelot turned and saw King Arthur. He lowered his sword. "My lord," he said.

"Leave Gawain," ordered Arthur. "You and I will fight."

Lancelot shook his head. "I will not," he whispered.

"Then you *are* a coward," said Arthur.

"I cannot fight you," pleaded Lancelot. "I have made a promise."

Lancelot dropped his sword to the ground. "I will not break this promise. I will not fight you."

Arthur raised his sword. "Then you will die!"

Sir Bors held his sword to Arthur's throat. "Shall I kill him and end the battle?" he asked.

Lancelot shook his head. "No. Arthur is our King. I don't want to hurt him." He helped Arthur to his feet.

Then he knelt down beside Gawain. "I am sorry, Gawain. I never meant this to happen." He pulled out a scarf and tried to stop Gawain's bleeding.

Lancelot turned to Arthur. "Order your knights to return to your camp. We will return to our castle." He picked up Arthur's sword and gave it back to him. "Tomorrow, we will talk."

Next morning, Lancelot and Guinevere looked down again from the castle walls.

Something was wrong. Arthur's camp was empty. The whole army had left during the night.

Guinevere sighed with relief. "They have gone. It is a miracle."

"No. Arthur would not just give up." Lancelot frowned. "Something must have happened."

Lancelot rode out of his castle. A messenger came towards him.

"Where is the King's army?" asked Lancelot.

"They have gone to fight Mordred," replied the messenger.

Lancelot stared at him. "Mordred?"

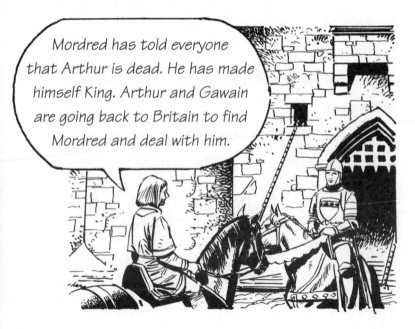

Arthur's army set sail for Britain. But the
journey was too much for Gawain. When he
reached land, he knew he was dying. He
asked to see the King.

"My lord," he groaned, "please forgive me. This is all my fault. Mordred should not have been left in charge. I forced you to leave Britain and fight Lancelot. I wanted revenge. I wanted Lancelot to die."

Arthur placed his hand on Gawain's shoulder.

"You are forgiven," he said.

"You must forgive Lancelot, too." Gawain tried to lift his head. "He is your greatest knight. Send for him. He will help you to defeat Mordred. Without him ..."

But he was too weak to finish the sentence. With those words, Gawain died.

CHAPTER 5

The final battle

Sir Gawain was buried. Then Arthur and his
army set off to meet Mordred. The armies
had agreed to fight on the field called
Camlann.

It was early in the morning. Mist drifted
across the field. The two armies stood facing
each other.

Mordred's army are
flying a flag of truce.

Arthur and Sir Bedivere looked across the field. A messenger rode out from Mordred's army.

Arthur watched him approach. "Perhaps Mordred has seen sense."

"Perhaps," said Bedivere.

The messenger continued. "Mordred will meet you in the middle of the field, half way between the two armies. Both sides may bring a small group of knights."

"It may be a trap," whispered Bedivere.

"I agree," said Arthur. "But if I do not go, brave knights will die."

He turned to the messenger.

Mordred's messenger rode away.

Bedivere frowned. "I will come with you," he said.

Arthur shook his head. "No, you stay here with the army. If Mordred has set a trap, I will order a knight to raise his sword. If you see the sword, sound the trumpets and begin the battle."

Later that day, Arthur met Mordred.

46

"Don't lie to me, Mordred," Arthur's voice was cold. "I know that you wish I was dead. I know that you want to be King."

Mordred's eye twitched.

"However, you are right," continued Arthur. "There has been too much fighting. We must have peace. So, I make this promise. Leave this field now and you will be King after my death."

Mordred smiled. He was a coward at heart. This way, he would be King without fighting. He nodded his head. "I agree. There will be peace."

As Mordred and Arthur shook hands, a snake slid out of the grass. It bit one of Arthur's knights on the ankle. The knight cried out and raised his sword to kill the snake.

It was too late. Back at Arthur's camp, Sir Bedivere saw the knight's sword flashing in the sunlight.

49

As the trumpets sounded, Arthur's knights began to advance. Mordred turned to Arthur. "You have lied!" he screamed. "You have broken the peace!"

Mordred drew his sword and gave the signal for his army to attack.

The final battle had begun.

Much later, as the sun set, two figures stood on a hill looking down on the battlefield. There was no sound. The dead lay in heaps.

"I am too late, Guinevere," Lancelot wept. "I have betrayed my King."

Guinevere turned to Lancelot. "This is my fault. I should not have fallen in love with you." Her eyes filled with tears. "I must not see you again."

Lancelot bowed his head. "Do you really mean what you say?" he asked.

"I do. I will go to a convent and become a nun."

Lancelot was silent. He looked down on the battlefield again.

"Then I shall become a priest," he said. "We must ask God for his forgiveness."

Lancelot took Guinevere's hand, and kissed it. Then, without a word, they turned and went their separate ways.

CHAPTER 6

The death of Arthur

As night fell, a voice called out across the
battlefield. "Arthur! My lord Arthur!"

King Arthur opened his eyes. His whole
body was a mass of pain. "Here!" he called
weakly.

Sir Bedivere limped towards the King, and
knelt beside him.

My lord.

"Bedivere," said Arthur, "where are the others?"

Bedivere's voice was full of grief. "There are no others, my lord. They are all dead." He pointed. "There lies Mordred, with your sword Excalibur through his heart."

The King groaned. "Then this is the end for me. But one more thing must be done."

Arthur gripped Bedivere's arm. Though the King was weak, his voice was stern. "There is a lake nearby. Take Excalibur, and throw it in the lake. Come back and tell me what you see."

Bedivere pulled Excalibur from Mordred's body. He took it to the lake.

Bedivere raised the sword to throw it into the lake. At the last moment, he stopped.

"I cannot do it," he thought. "Excalibur means too much. I cannot throw it away."

He hid the sword under some bushes, and went back to Arthur.

The King opened his eyes. "Did you throw Excalibur into the lake?" he asked.

"Yes, my lord," said Bedivere.

"What did you see?"

"I saw nothing but the wind and waves."

"Then you have lied to me," said Arthur gently. "Do as I ask."

Bedivere was ashamed. He went back to the lake and picked up the hidden sword.

He stood on the bank. Then with all his strength, Bedivere threw Excalibur out across the lake.

But the sword never hit the water.

Bedivere returned to the dying King. He told Arthur what he had seen.

Arthur gave a deep sigh. "The Lady of the Lake has her sword again. My kingdom is at an end."

"I will go and find help for you," said Bedivere.

But Arthur shook his head. "Take off my helmet and carry me to the lake."

A boat floated by the water's edge. Three women stood in the boat, waiting silently. They were dressed in black robes with black hoods.

Bedivere laid the King in the boat and stepped back onto the bank.

The boat drifted away, over the lake. One of the women placed Arthur's head in her lap. The women began to sing. Their soft voices carried over the water.

Bedivere felt that his heart was breaking. "Where are they taking you?" he cried.

"I am going to be healed." The King's voice sounded young and strong again. "Then I shall sleep. But I will return when the world needs me again."

Sir Bedivere watched the boat until it was out of sight.

The final battle was over.

ABOUT THE AUTHORS

Steve Skidmore and Steve Barlow live in the Midlands and teach drama. They also write together.

Skidmore writes the consonants, and Barlow writes the vowels. They are always arguing about punctuation.

Despite this, they have written many books and plays, including a number in the *Impact* series. They have also written several other novels for teenagers, including *The Lost Diaries* series and *The Mad Myths* series.

RETELLING
SET C